American Gi

A Girl Named
Hillary

The True Story of
HILLARY D. R. CLINTON

By **Rebecca Paley**

Illustrated by **Melissa Manwill**

Scholastic Inc.

Published by Scholastic Inc., *Publishers since 1920.* SCHOLASTIC and associated logos are trademarks and/or registered trademarks of Scholastic Inc. The publisher does not have any control over and does not assume any responsibility for author or third-party websites or their content.

Photos ©: 43 top: Clinton Press Office PubImages/Newscom; 43 bottom: Wellesley College/Getty Images; 44: Ira Wyman/Getty Images; 45 top: New York *Daily News* Archive/Getty Images; 45 bottom: dpa picture alliance archive/Alamy Images; 46: Justin Lane/Epa/REX/Shutterstock; 47: Tom Belair.

Book design by Suzanne LaGasa

Library of Congress Cataloging-in-Publication Data Available

ISBN 978-1-338-19302-2

10 9 8 7 6 5 4 3 2 1   18 19 20 21 22

Printed in the U.S.A.   23
First printing 2018

Contents

Introduction

On a warm night in July 2016, Hillary Clinton stood in front of a cheering crowd in Philadelphia. She had just accepted the **nomination** of the Democratic Party to run for president of the United States of America. This was the first time that a woman had been chosen by a major political party to run for president. Hillary knew this was an important moment in history, especially for women. She said during her acceptance speech, "I'm so happy this day has come . . . because when any barrier falls in America, for anyone, it clears the way for everyone."

Growing up, Hillary believed that she could do anything she put her mind to. And she was right!

Chapter 1

Growing Up in Park Ridge

Hillary Diane Rodham was born in Chicago on October 26, 1947. When she was three years old, her parents moved from the city to Park Ridge, Illinois. Park Ridge was a nice neighborhood with lots of trees and families.

Hillary grew up with her two younger brothers, Hugh Jr. and Tony. Their dad, Hugh, was a very hard worker. Hugh expected his children to help out around the house. The three kids always had a long list of chores. He was also careful about money. Hillary and her brothers didn't get new clothes often.

Hillary's mom, Dorothy, stayed at home to take care of the children. She wanted her young daughter to be strong and brave. When Hillary was four years old, her mom noticed she wasn't outside playing with the other kids. Dorothy asked her daughter why she was sitting alone in the house, and Hillary started to cry.

Hillary explained that a girl named Suzy had been bullying her and she was afraid to go outside.

Dorothy encouraged Hillary to march outside and face Suzy. "You have to stand up for yourself," she said. "There's no room in this house for cowards."

Hillary must have been scared, but she stood up to Suzy, just as her mother instructed. She learned never to back down from a challenge.

Chapter 2

Do All the Good You Can

Hillary's mom also taught her the importance of helping people who were poor or less **fortunate**. Dorothy often repeated something they heard in church: "Do all the good you can, for all the people you can, in all the ways you can."

Hillary remembered this message when their church asked for **volunteers** to babysit the children of Mexican farmworkers in their community. Although she was only eleven years old, she raised her hand. Along with a couple of her friends, Hillary went to her church after school to help take care of the children. Spending time with these families, Hillary realized how fortunate she and her friends were to have money.

At twelve years old, Hillary organized a backyard carnival to raise money for a **charity** that helped poor people pay for food, shelter, and other things they needed. Kids from all over her neighborhood paid to play games and sports at the carnival. The money raised was given to the United Way. The event was such a hit that the local newspaper printed a story about it!

Hillary worked hard at whatever she did. As a Brownie and a Girl Scout, she earned many **merit badges**. At school, she worked hard to get straight As.

Education was very important to her family. Dorothy wanted her children to learn through reading books. She took Hillary to the library every week. Hillary loved working her way through the books in the children's section.

Chapter 3

Being a Girl

Hillary worked just as hard at things she wasn't naturally good at—like baseball. She loved playing baseball, but because her vision was poor, she had a lot of trouble hitting the ball. She didn't give up, though. Hugh spent hours pitching balls to his daughter until she learned to hit.

Hugh included Hillary in all of the activities he did with his sons. That included fishing, shooting tin cans, and playing sports during summer vacations at the family's cabin in Pennsylvania.

From a young age, Hillary was very ambitious. One of her greatest dreams was to become an **astronaut**. When Hillary was little, she and her brother Hugh used to pretend they were on missions to Mars—with Hillary at the controls.

When she was fourteen, Hillary sent a letter to the National Aeronautics and Space Administration (NASA). She wanted to find out how she could get into an astronaut-training program.

NASA's answer? She couldn't—because she was a girl. At that time, women astronauts

didn't exist, and the government had no plans to change that.

The news came as a big shock to Hillary, who had been raised to believe she could do anything. This wasn't the last time that she was treated unfairly just because she was a girl.

Chapter 4

Winning and Losing

Hillary was also interested in the student **government** at her high school. This was a group of kids chosen by their classmates to try to make the school better. After she was **elected** vice president of her junior class, Hillary decided to run for class president during her senior year. She was disappointed when she lost. She was even more upset when the winner told her she lost because she was a girl.

Hillary didn't give up. She went off to Wellesley College, an all-female school outside of Boston, and got right back into student government. First, she was chosen as a class

representative. A representative is someone chosen to speak for others. Three years later, she ran for president of the student government and won!

Hillary fought for students to have more choice in the kinds of classes they could take.

She supported having more African American students and professors at the school. She won these battles by talking with and standing up to the adult leaders who ran the college.

Fighting for her classmates wasn't the only way she stood up for what she believed in. In 1969, Hillary was the first student ever to speak at the Wellesley graduation ceremony. She could have used her time on stage to praise herself or the college. Instead, she talked about problems that continued to exist in the United States, such as poverty. No one expected a woman to be so outspoken.

Like the little girl who stood up to the neighborhood bully, Hillary showed courage by being bold during her speech. It was so powerful, it made the news! She was talked about in newspapers and on TV throughout the country.

Chapter 5

Lawyer, Mother, First Lady

After college, Hillary attended law school at Yale University. At that time, many people thought women should be homemakers, teachers, or nurses, not **lawyers**. Hillary disagreed. She knew that as a lawyer she could fight for fairness and help people in need. She met her future husband, Bill Clinton, in one of her law school classes.

Bill and Hillary were married in Arkansas in 1975. She joined the Rose Law Firm a year later, and Bill went on to become the governor of Arkansas. The two became parents when their daughter, Chelsea, was born in 1980.

Hillary continued to work as a lawyer after Chelsea was born. Throughout her career,

Hillary loved children and wanted to help them. Her first job out of law school was for the Children's Defense Fund, an organization that helps children in need. She went door-to-door to find out why a lot of kids, especially those with **disabilities**, were missing so much school. The information she gathered led to a brand-new law requiring public schools to do a better job of educating these students.

As a lawyer, Hillary also took on a lot of cases for children, even if their families couldn't afford to pay her.

When Bill became president in 1993, the Clintons moved from Arkansas to the White House. As first lady, Hillary wanted to fight for families who needed help. She tried to make it possible for millions of Americans to afford to go to the doctor. She supported programs to help children get a better education. She spoke out against violence toward women and became a champion for women's rights around the world.

Chapter 6

Never Give Up

After eight years as first lady, Hillary became one of just thirteen women in the US Senate. A **senator** is someone chosen from their state to help make laws. Hillary was the first wife of a president to be elected to the Senate and the first female senator from New York. She worked in the Senate for eight years before running for president in 2008 as the Democratic nominee. Hillary lost the first stage of the election, the **primary**, and Senator Barack Obama was chosen to run instead.

Soon after Obama was elected president, he asked her to be his **secretary of state**. In this important government job, Hillary helped countries around the world try to solve problems. She fought for women's rights and worked to improve the lives of people in poorer countries that didn't have enough food or access to medical care. In four years, Hillary visited 112 countries, more than any other secretary of state in history!

Although Hillary always gives her all to everything she does, that doesn't mean she always succeeds. She ran again for president of the United States in 2016 and didn't win. Even though she lost the election, her nomination was still an enormous victory for women.

Hillary wanted young people in particular to know the importance of believing in themselves. The lesson she wanted to focus on after her defeat was this: Whether you've won or lost, never, ever give up.

"To all the little girls who are watching this," she said after the election, "never doubt that you are valuable and powerful and deserving of every chance and opportunity in the world to pursue and achieve your own dreams."

GLOSSARY

ASTRONAUT: someone who travels in space

CHARITY: an organization that helps people in need

DISABILITY: the lack of ability, strength, or power to do something

ELECT: to choose someone or decide something by voting

FORTUNATE: having good luck or wealth

GOVERNMENT: a group that controls and manages a country, state, city, or organization

LAWYER: a person trained to advise people about the law and speak for them in court

MERIT BADGE: a pin or patch earned for doing something good

NOMINATION: the act of choosing a person to run for office

PRIMARY: an election to choose a candidate who will run in the general election

REPRESENTATIVE: someone who is chosen to speak or act for others

SECRETARY OF STATE: an important government official who manages America's relationships with other countries

SENATOR: someone elected to help make laws for their state

VOLUNTEER: someone who offers to do a job, usually without pay

TIMELINE

1947: Hillary Diane Rodham is born in Chicago, Illinois, on October 26

1950: The Rodham family moves to Park Ridge, Illinois

1959: Hillary organizes a backyard carnival to raise money for the United Way

A childhood portrait of Hillary

1968: Hillary is elected president of the student government at Wellesley College

Hillary Rodham at Wellesley College, 1969

1969: In May, Hillary graduates from Wellesley College and becomes the first student to give a speech during the ceremony

1969: Hillary begins Yale Law School in August

1973: Hillary begins working for the Children's Defense Fund

1975: Hillary marries Bill Clinton

1978: Hillary becomes first lady of Arkansas when Bill Clinton is elected governor of Arkansas

1980: Daughter Chelsea is born

1993: Hillary becomes first lady of the United States when Bill Clinton becomes president

First Lady Hillary Clinton with her husband, President Bill Clinton, and their daughter, Chelsea

2000: Hillary is elected as first female senator from New York

2006: Hillary is reelected to the Senate for second term

2008: Hillary loses Democratic primary election to Barack Obama

2009: Hillary is appointed secretary of state

Senator Hillary Clinton greets students on Earth Day, April 22, 2002.

Secretary of State Hillary Clinton with President Barack Obama at a meeting in France, April 4, 2009

Hillary Clinton accepting the Democratic nomination to run for president of the United States

2016: In July, Hillary accepts the Democratic nomination to run for president of the United States

2016: Hillary loses the election to Donald Trump in November

2017: Hillary speaks at the Women in the World Summit in New York City

A GIRL NAMED ALENA

There are a lot of young girls helping to make positive changes in our world today, just like Hillary Clinton did. Alena Mulhern is one of those girls.

My mom always told me that when I grow up, I could be whatever I wanted. When I was seven, I told her I wanted to be president of the United States one day. That's when she gave me the bad news. Only people born in the United States can be president. I'm American, but I was born in China. My parents adopted me when I was a baby.

I was disappointed that an unfair law would keep me from my dream. Then I thought, *Hey wait! This is America.* We all have the right to use our voice and try to change things we believe are unfair.

I learned how our government works and how laws are created or changed. Then I asked all my classmates and teachers to sign a petition saying they believed in my cause.

I shared the petition (I got 120 signatures!) with lawmakers in my state, asking them to support my cause, too. The Massachusetts State House filed a resolution on my behalf and asked me to testify (which means to speak) in person. To prepare, I typed what I wanted to say. I practiced over and over again in front of my family. On the day of my speech, I brought notes with me. I felt prepared. I'm still waiting to hear whether the resolution passes. If it does, it will go to Congress for consideration. If the resolution doesn't pass, you can bet I'll keep trying.